THE JIM CROW ERA

by Kathleen M. Muldoon

COLORED
WAITING ROOM
INTRASTATE PASSENGERS

WITHDRAWN

Content Consultant
Ibram X. Kendi, PhD
Assistant Professor, Africana Studies Department
University at Albany, SUNY

Core Library

An Imprint of Abdo Publishing
www.abdopublishing.com

Published by Abdo Publishing, a division of ABDO, PO Box 398166,
Minneapolis, Minnesota 55439. Copyright © 2015 by Abdo Consulting
Group, Inc. International copyrights reserved in all countries. No part of
this book may be reproduced in any form without written permission from
the publisher. Core Library™ is a trademark and logo of Abdo Publishing.

Printed in the United States of America,
North Mankato, Minnesota
022014
092014

Editor: Holly Saari
Series Designer: Becky Daum

Library of Congress Cataloging-in-Publication Data
Muldoon, Kathleen M.
   The Jim Crow Era / by Kathleen M. Muldoon.
      pages cm. -- (African American History)
   ISBN 978-1-62403-146-5
1. African Americans--Segregation--Southern States--History--Juvenile
literature. 2. African Americans--Civil rights--Southern States--History--
Juvenile literature. 3. Southern States--Race relations--History--Juvenile
literature. I. Title.
   E185.61.M955 2014
   323.1196'073075--dc23
                           2013027632

Photo Credits: Bettmann/Corbis/AP Images, cover, 1; North Wind/North
Wind Picture Archives, 4, 6, 9, 10, 25; AP Images, 14, 18, 33; Marion Post
Wolcott/Library of Congress/Getty Images, 17; Buyenlarge/Getty Images,
20; Rudolph Faircloth/AP Images, 23, 45; Frances Benjamin Johnston/
Library of Congress, 28; U.S. Army Signal Corps/Library of Congress, 30;
Red Line Editorial, 35, 40; Library of Congress, 36; U.S. Army Signal Corps/
AP Images, 39

CONTENTS

CHAPTER ONE

RECONSTRUCTION CRUMBLES

In 1607 English settlers founded the first British colony in North America. In 1619 a ship carrying Africans arrived in the colony. They were sold as slaves. The white colonists thought these Africans were beneath them because their skin was darker. Whites forced the slaves to live and work on their land. The slaves worked from morning to night

Slavery lasted in the United States for more than 200 years.

Once slavery ended, former slaves needed to find housing and jobs.

without pay. Those who refused to work or tried to run away were beaten or killed.

Slavery Ends

By 1860 approximately 4 million slaves lived in the United States. Most were forced to work on plantations and farms in the South. Slavery was one of several issues that led to the American Civil War in 1861. The North wanted to ban slavery in new territories. The South wanted these areas to be able to have slavery. The war ended in 1865. The Northern states won. The Thirteenth Amendment was added to the US Constitution in 1865. It ended slavery in the United States.

The period after the war was called Reconstruction. During this time the government worked to reunite the Northern and Southern states. The government also addressed how freed slaves would be treated. Congress passed the Civil Rights Act of 1875. The act made sure African Americans were treated equally in public places. These included schools and libraries. The act also kept some private businesses from discriminating against African Americans.

The government sent troops to the South to protect African Americans.

The Fourteenth Amendment

The Fourteenth Amendment was added to the US Constitution in 1868. This Reconstruction amendment stated that African Americans were equal citizens of the United States. They had all the rights protected by the Constitution. They could live, work, worship, and travel as freely as white people could.

But the troops could not change the attitudes of white Americans. Whites kept African Americans from getting land, wealth, or education. They used physical force and violence to do so. This kept the former slaves poor.

Losing Political Power

In 1870 African-American men gained the right to vote. They helped elect Republican President Rutherford B. Hayes in 1877. But the election was very close. Democrats in the South made a compromise in order to go along with the election results. Hayes would become president. But he would support Democrats in power in southern

Political Parties

During Reconstruction the Republican Party supported equal rights for African Americans. It helped many African Americans run for political office. Several won their elections too. But southern Democrats were against African-American political power. The Democrats regained power in the South. Then they stopped African Americans from running for political office.

African Americans usually voted for Republicans, who believed African Americans should be treated equally.

states. He would also remove the troops that were in the South. This was the end of Reconstruction.

White Democratic politicians again gained power once the soldiers left. Many Democrats believed African Americans should not have the same freedoms

Southern white Democrats wanted to go back to a time when African Americans had no rights.

as whites. African Americans again had their rights taken away and were prevented from improving their lives.

The Redeemers were a group of Democrats. They wanted to return to the days before the Civil War when white people controlled the lives of African Americans. They wanted to take away the power and equality African Americans had gained under the new laws. The Redeemers began taking over southern state governments. They passed laws that separated white and African-American citizens. They raised taxes. They lowered cotton prices. African Americans who had gained land lost it. Redeemers decreased African-American voting power. African Americans were forced to pass difficult or impossible tests before they could vote.

No More Civil Rights Act

The Civil Rights Act of 1875 stood in the way of the Redeemers' goals. How could the Redeemers take away African Americans' freedoms without breaking this law? Some white business owners decided to test the law. They did not let African Americans into their businesses.

Some African Americans sued the business owners for this. Those cases ended up in the US Supreme Court. In 1883 the Supreme Court ruled that the Civil Rights Act of 1875 was unconstitutional. The Court ruled that the Fourteenth Amendment did not apply to discrimination by privately owned businesses.

African Americans suffered because of this Supreme Court ruling. The government could no longer protect the civil rights of newly freed slaves. Whites who did not believe African Americans were equal to them held economic and political power in the southern states. African Americans' lives remained limited by severe discrimination and inequality.

Justice John Harlan was the only member of the Supreme Court who voted to keep the Civil Rights Act of 1875. This white justice wrote,

> *Today, it is the colored race which is denied, by corporations and individuals wielding public authority, rights fundamental in their freedom and citizenship. At some future time, it may be some other race will fall under the ban of race discrimination. If the constitutional amendments be enforced . . . there cannot be in this republic, any class of human beings in practical subjection to another class.*

Source: *"Civil Rights Cases, 1883."* Encylopedia.com. *HighBeam Research, Inc., 1997. Web. Accessed June 11, 2013.*

Nice View

Read this passage closely. Then reread Chapter One to see how white people felt about African Americans after slavery ended. How does Justice Harlan's passage shed new light on these views? Write a short essay comparing the two points of view.

CHAPTER TWO

SEPARATE AND UNEQUAL

The Jim Crow era began when Reconstruction ended in 1877. Southern states passed laws that made segregation a way of life. The laws became known as Jim Crow laws. These laws forced African Americans to be separated from whites. White southern politicians said African Americans would still get equal treatment under the Fourteenth Amendment. But this did not happen. African

Jim Crow laws kept African Americans separate from whites in public spaces, such as public transportation waiting rooms.

Americans faced worse living conditions than whites. Many whites used Jim Crow laws to keep African Americans under their power.

So Many Laws

The first major Jim Crow law passed in 1890 in New Orleans, Louisiana. The city stated African Americans could not ride in the same railroad cars as white people. Instead they could travel only in cars for "coloreds." These cars were usually dirty. Sometimes the cars were even shared by animals being sent to the butcher.

Most of the laws ordered businesses and public places to keep white people and African Americans separate. Restaurants could not serve food to whites and African Americans in the

The Term Jim Crow

Jim Crow laws were named for a character created by a white actor in 1828. The actor blackened his face. He played a character named Jim Crow. Jim Crow was a racist caricature of an African American. Jim Crow became a negative term for African Americans.

Facilities for African Americans were often inferior to those of whites.

same room. Whites and African Americans could not play any game together. White and African-American children could not attend the same schools. An African-American barber could not cut the hair of white women or girls. Employers had to provide separate bathrooms for white and African-American men. Other laws stated African Americans could not date, marry, or touch whites.

Local and state governments in the South made so many Jim Crow laws it was hard to keep track of them. The Jim Crow laws were different in each city

Some public places excluded African Americans unless they were maids or other workers.

and state. African Americans who moved had to learn what they could and could not do in their new city.

Fighting Back

In 1892 a group of African Americans wanted to challenge Louisiana's law about segregated trains. They called themselves the American Citizens' Equal Rights Association. They arranged for Homer Plessy to board a train and sit in the white section. Plessy was arrested for breaking the law. The group hired a lawyer to defend him. The lawyer argued in the courts that Plessy had been denied his equal treatment under the law.

The Supreme Court ruled against Plessy in 1896 in *Plessy v. Ferguson*. The Court stated that facilities could be segregated by race. Each group just had to have equal facilities. This "separate but equal" ruling caused segregation to spread. Southern states passed even more Jim Crow laws. Even though facilities were supposed to be equal, lawmakers got around this. Places for African Americans were shabby and run-down. African Americans were treated as separate but not equal to whites.

CHAPTER THREE

LIVING IN THE SHADOWS

Jim Crow laws were almost everywhere African Americans and whites came together. Signs reminded African Americans that white people considered them secondary. Bus signs told African Americans they had to sit in the back. Some hospitals, hotels, parks, and public buildings had one entrance for whites. They had another for African Americans. Signs even told African Americans which water

African-American children had to follow Jim Crow laws as well.

fountains they could drink from. Other places left out African Americans altogether.

Slavery may have ended decades before. But African Americans in the South were not free. Many former slaves worked for former slave owners. The white employers gave the hardest jobs to African-American employees. African Americans were paid lower wages than the white employees who did the easiest work.

Woman Power

African-American women were sources of strength for their families during the Jim Crow era. African-American women in northern and southern states began to form clubs during this time. In 1896 many of these clubs joined forces. They formed the National Association of Colored Women (NACW). The NACW worked to end discrimination. It also worked to end poverty among African Americans. By 1914 the NACW had 50,000 members.

Growing Up under Jim Crow

It was not against the law for young children of different races to play together. But white children and African-American children had

African-American students attended separate schools from whites, and their schools had fewer resources.

separate playgrounds, schools, and parks. Facilities were not equal either. Local governments made the public spaces for white children better than those for African-American children. Playgrounds for African Americans were often weedy corner lots. They had broken-down swings and slides. Schools had few books or supplies. White children had new playground equipment. They had plenty of books and supplies at school.

African-American children learned what the Jim Crow laws wanted them to think. Many grew up thinking white people were better than them. African-American parents had to work hard to fight against this. To keep their children safe, they taught them to obey the Jim Crow laws. Many also taught their children pride in being African-American. They might be secondary in the eyes of the law. But they were not secondary in truth.

Cycle of Poverty

African Americans received poorer educations than whites. Employers used this as an excuse. They refused to hire African Americans for jobs. Or they paid them poorly

Jobs during Jim Crow

Jim Crow laws made it very difficult for African Americans to get good-paying jobs. Some jobs were only allowed for whites. A few African Americans in the South owned their own businesses. Some farmed their own land. But most worked for white factory owners or farmers. African Americans picked crops. They built roads and cleaned buildings. Some washed dishes or linens in restaurants or hotels. African-American women worked as servants in white homes or hotels. African Americans often worked from sunup to sundown.

African Americans sometimes worked for their former slave owners and earned little pay.

and gave them difficult jobs. Often a white person who could not do a job well was hired instead of an African American who could do the job well. The system of racist laws and practices made sure African Americans stayed poor no matter how hard they worked. African Americans had no say in government. Much of their time was spent trying to follow the Jim Crow laws.

Unjust Crimes and Punishment

Punishment for breaking Jim Crow laws was as unjust as the laws themselves. White people ran the police and court systems. An African-American man who forgot to tip his hat to a white person could be fined or put in prison. Some laws applied to white people who tried to help African Americans. One ordered white teachers to pay a fine for teaching African-American students.

The harshest act under Jim Crow was lynching. This was often when a white mob hung an African American. Whites who performed these acts used them to intimidate African Americans. The white people wanted to make sure African Americans followed Jim Crow laws and did not protest for change. During the Jim Crow era of 1877 to 1954, more than 3,500 African Americans were lynched by white mobs.

Ida B. Wells-Barnett was an African-American teacher and writer. She wrote about what happened to her in 1884. She was sitting in the white coach section of a train in Tennessee:

> *When the train started and the conductor came along to collect tickets, he . . . told me I would have to go in the other car. I refused, saying that the forward car was a smoker, and as I was in the ladies car I proposed to stay. . . . He went forward and got the baggage-man and another man to help him and of course they succeeded in dragging me out. They were encouraged to do this by the attitude of the white ladies and gentlemen in the car; some of them even stood on the seats so that they could get a good view and continued applauding the conductor for his brave stand.*
>
> Source: Ida B. Wells-Barnett. "I Had Braced My Feet." TN History for Kids! *Tennessee History for Kids, Inc.*, n.d. Web. Accessed July 15, 2013.

What's the Big Idea?

Read the above passage carefully. What is Wells-Barnett's main point in telling about this event? Pick out two details that support this point. What can you tell about what it was like for African Americans to live under Jim Crow laws?

CHAPTER FOUR

INTO THE TWENTIETH CENTURY

B y the early 1900s, southern African Americans had faced harsh Jim Crow laws for decades. Yet they still had hopes and dreams for their future. Some African-American families and communities thrived. African-American writers, such as Langston Hughes, began recording their proud heritage and culture.

In the early 1900s, Booker T. Washington became a leader in education by helping train African Americans for better jobs.

W. E. B. Du Bois believed college education, not job training, was the best way for African Americans to get out of poverty.

Focus on Education

African-American leaders pressed for better education for African Americans. One was Booker T. Washington. By 1900 the former slave was considered one of the top African-American leaders. He started programs that trained African Americans for jobs on farms and in factories.

W. E. B. Du Bois thought job training alone would keep southern African Americans under the control of Jim Crow laws. He believed the best way for them to rise up was through college education. In 1905 Du Bois and other African-American leaders worked for the right to get a college education. Most colleges in the southern states and in some northern states were segregated. Several kept African Americans out completely. Some colleges were specifically for African Americans. These colleges taught African-American students trades such as farming rather than traditional college courses. African-American groups began asking Congress to improve college education

Testing Voters

The Fifteenth Amendment gave African-American men the right to vote in 1870. During the Jim Crow era, voting officials often made African Americans pass literacy tests before they could vote. Those who failed were thought unable to understand the ballot. Even if they got every question right, an official might say it took them too long to answer. Then they could not vote.

for African Americans. They wanted more resources for their education. By the end of the Jim Crow era, African-American students received more resources.

African-American Power vs. White Violence

In 1908 a mob of whites in Springfield, Illinois, randomly attacked a group of African Americans. Two African Americans were killed. Many more were hurt. Many white and African-American leaders were shocked by this hatred and violence. They met to discuss ways to stop it. In 1909 these leaders formed the National Association for the Advancement of Colored People (NAACP). Its goal was to make sure all races had civil rights. It also wanted to end prejudice. By 1919 the NAACP had 90,000 members.

In the South, groups such as the White Brotherhood noticed African Americans organizing. They saw this organizing as a threat to their goal of making sure whites ruled the South. One of the most violent groups was the Ku Klux Klan (KKK). During

KKK members wore masks to hide their true identities from the African Americans they intimidated.

Reconstruction its members killed African Americans and whites who backed them. In the early 1900s, the KKK threatened African Americans.

The Great Migration

Ninety percent of African Americans lived in the South in 1900. In 1916 many started moving to northern and western states. By 1920 approximately 1 million African Americans had moved out of the South.

The Chicago Defender

African-American writer and editor Robert S. Abbott began publishing a newspaper for African Americans in 1905. It was known as the *Chicago Defender*. The paper told of the horrible violence toward African Americans. Information in the newspaper about northern states was helpful to southern African Americans during the Great Migration.

This was due to the increasing violence by white hate groups. African Americans also hoped to escape poverty. They hoped to get better housing and education in the North. Big cities in the North had better jobs for African Americans. They could work in factories.

This period of movement is called the Great Migration. It lasted until 1970. African Americans in northern and western states still faced discrimination. Schools were still segregated. But there were fewer Jim Crow laws in those states.

However, many northern whites were prejudiced against African Americans. Landlords rented to

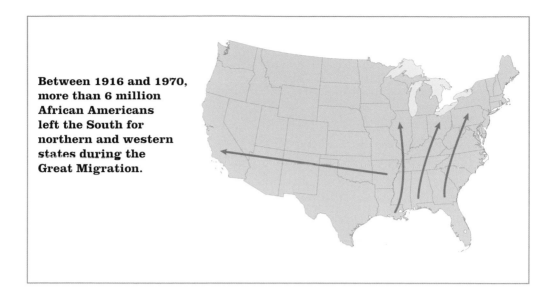

Between 1916 and 1970, more than 6 million African Americans left the South for northern and western states during the Great Migration.

Migration Routes

This map shows the major routes taken by African Americans during the Great Migration. What are two changes African Americans might have encountered after moving to cities in northern and western states?

African Americans only in the poorest parts of the city. Employers could say African Americans did not have enough education to work for them. Some African Americans who moved to northern states were able to climb out of poverty. But many found themselves in the same or worse situations they had left in the South.

CHAPTER FIVE

JIM CROW ENDS

Soon other events led to major changes in the lives of African Americans. One was World War I (1914–1918). In 1917 President Woodrow Wilson sent US troops to Europe. They went to help England and other countries fight Germany. African Americans were among the first to volunteer to fight. Even in war, though, African Americans were kept separate from whites.

African-American soldiers fought in segregated units during World War I.

The Tuskegee Airmen

African Americans were not allowed to be military pilots until World War II. White military officials considered African Americans not intelligent enough to fly aircraft. In 1941 African-American civil rights leaders pressured the War Department. They wanted the department to begin a pilot training program for African Americans. It was held in Tuskegee, Alabama. The 992 men who graduated were known as the Tuskegee Airmen. These pilots served overseas in World War II. They proved themselves as good as white pilots.

Another War

When World War II (1939–1945) broke out in Europe, African Americans believed it would not be long before the United States became involved in the fighting. Before that happened, they wanted the government to end segregation in the military. In 1941 President Franklin Roosevelt signed an order. It stated that all soldiers could fully take part in the military no matter their "race, creed, color, or national origin." This order let African Americans

The Tuskegee Airmen fought bravely during
World War II.

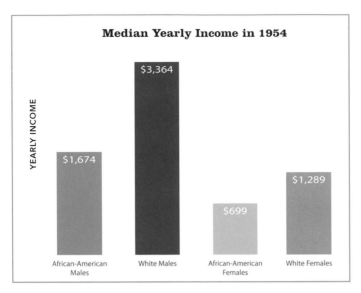

Median Yearly Income in 1954

YEARLY INCOME

- African-American Males: $1,674
- White Males: $3,364
- African-American Females: $699
- White Females: $1,289

Inequality of Pay

This chart compares the yearly income of African Americans and whites at the end of the Jim Crow era. This book discusses the types of jobs open to African Americans during this time. Are the differences in income what you imagined? Why do you think women of both races earned less than men did in 1954?

challenge racism in the military. But the order did not do away with segregation.

Another Supreme Court Decision

In 1954 the US Supreme Court heard another case involving segregation. Linda Brown and several other African-American students had been told they could not attend white schools. The Supreme Court ruled this was unconstitutional. It stated that separate

EXPLORE ONLINE

The focus of Chapter Five is the changes African Americans faced in the 1900s. The chapter also details the end of the Jim Crow era. The website below discusses the *Brown v. Board of Education* case. As you know, every source is different. How is the information given in the website different from the information in this chapter? What information is the same? How do the two sources present information differently?

Landmark Cases: *Brown v. Board of Education* (1954)
www.mycorelibrary.com/jim-crow-era

education was not equal education. The Court ordered that public schools in the United States must be open to students of all races. This ruling marked the end of the Jim Crow era.

The *Brown v. Board of Education* decision did not immediately end violence and discrimination toward African Americans. But it did open the courts to African Americans to fight Jim Crow and other laws that took away their equal rights.

IMPORTANT DATES

1619

The first slaves arrive in the British colonies of the present-day United States.

1865

Slavery in the United States is abolished.

1877

Reconstruction ends and the Jim Crow era begins.

1896

African-American women form the NACW to fight racial injustice.

1909

African-American leaders form the NAACP.

1916

African Americans in the South begin moving to northern and western states during the Great Migration.

1883

1890

1896

The Supreme Court rules that the Civil Rights Act of 1875 is unconstitutional.

New Orleans passes the first major Jim Crow law forbidding African Americans to ride in the same trains as white people.

The Supreme Court upholds New Orleans' law ordering segregated passenger trains in *Plessy v. Ferguson.*

1929

1941

1954

The Great Depression begins. It especially affects poor African Americans.

President Roosevelt signs an order that protects the rights of African Americans to enlist in the military.

The Supreme Court ruling in *Brown v. Board of Education* ends the Jim Crow era.

STOP AND THINK

Tell the Tale

Chapter Three contains a story of what happened to Ida B. Wells-Barnett when she boarded a train. Write 200 words that tell her story in detail. Describe what she saw and heard as the conductor and other men dragged her off the train. Be sure to set the scene, develop a sequence of events, and offer a conclusion.

Dig Deeper

After reading this book, what questions do you still have about the Jim Crow era? Write down one or two questions that can guide you in doing research. With an adult's help, find a few reliable sources about this time period that can help answer your questions. Write a few sentences about how you did your research and what you learned from it.

Why Do I Care?

The Jim Crow era came to an end more than 50 years ago. But you can still relate that time period to today. Do you see unfair treatment happening today? What did you learn from this book that can help fix those situations?

Take a Stand

This book discusses Jim Crow laws. Do you think the courts should have allowed these laws to continue as long as they did? Why or why not? Write a short essay explaining your opinion. Make sure to give reasons for your opinion.

GLOSSARY

amendment
an addition or change made to an existing law or legal document

discriminate
to treat someone unfairly based on differences such as race or gender

heritage
the valued history and traditions of a culture or group of people

lynch
to put someone to death, often by hanging, by a mob of people

migrate
to move from one area to another

prejudice
hatred or unfair treatment due to having fixed opinions about a group of people

segregate
to involuntarily separate or keep people apart from another group

troops
soldiers

unconstitutional
not in agreement with the constitution of a government

LEARN MORE

Books

Haskins, James, and Kathleen Benson. *The Rise of Jim Crow*. Tarrytown, NY: Marshall Cavendish Benchmark, 2008.

Morrison, Toni. *Remember: The Journey to School Integration*. Boston: Houghton Mifflin, 2004.

Websites

To learn more about African-American History, visit **booklinks.abdopublishing.com**. These links are routinely monitored and updated to provide the most current information available. Visit **www.mycorelibrary.com** for free additional tools for teachers and students.

INDEX

ABOUT THE AUTHOR

Kathleen M. Muldoon is a retired journalist. Currently, she teaches adult writing courses and workshops. She has written several books for educational publishers as well as numerous stories and magazine articles for adults and children.